spot

OUTDOOR FUN

HIKING

by Nessa Black

AMICUS | AMICUS INK

backpack

map

Look for these words and pictures as you read.

sign

compass

It is a nice day.
Let's go for a hike!

backpack

Do you see the backpack?

It carries water and snacks.

Jen takes along trail mix.

Do you see the map?
It shows the trails.
It tells how far we can hike.

map

The trail is rocky.
It can be hard to walk.
We wear good boots.

Do you see the sign?
It tells us to watch for bears.
They can be dangerous.

sign

BEAR

X-ING

Do you see the compass?
It helps us find the way.
It shows which way is north.

compass

Evan stops to rest.
How far will he hike?

spot

Spot is published by Amicus and Amicus Ink
P.O. Box 1329, Mankato, MN 56002
www.amicuspublishing.us

Library of Congress Cataloging-in-Publication Data
Names: Black, Nessa, author.
Title: Hiking / by Nessa Black.
Description: Mankato, Minnesota : Amicus/Amicus Ink,
 [2020] | Series: Spot outdoor fun | Audience: Grades:
 K to Grade 3.
Identifiers: LCCN 2019003796 (print) | LCCN
 2019015195 (ebook) | ISBN 9781681518527 (pdf) | ISBN
 9781681518121 (library binding) | ISBN 9781681525402
 (pbk.) | ISBN 9781681518527 (ebook)
Subjects: LCSH: Hiking--Juvenile literature. | Vocabulary--
 Juvenile literature.
Classification: LCC GV199.52 (ebook) | LCC GV199.52 .B53
 2020 (print) | DDC 796.51--dc23
LC record available at https://lccn.loc.gov/2019003796

Printed in China

HC 10 9 8 7 6 5 4 3 2 1
PB 10 9 8 7 6 5 4 3 2 1

Wendy Dieker, editor
Deb Miner, series designer
Aubrey Harper, book designer
Shane Freed, photo researcher

Photos by jazz42/iStock cover;
Alexander Raths/Shutterstock 1, 16;
Monkey Business Images/Shutterstock 3;
Maridav/Shutterstock 4–5; FatCamera/
iStock 6–7; gaspr13/iStock 8–9; Radius
Images/Alamy 10–11; PhotoMelon/
iStock 12–13; Max Topchii/Shutterstock
14–15